NYC

This journal belongs to

Notes

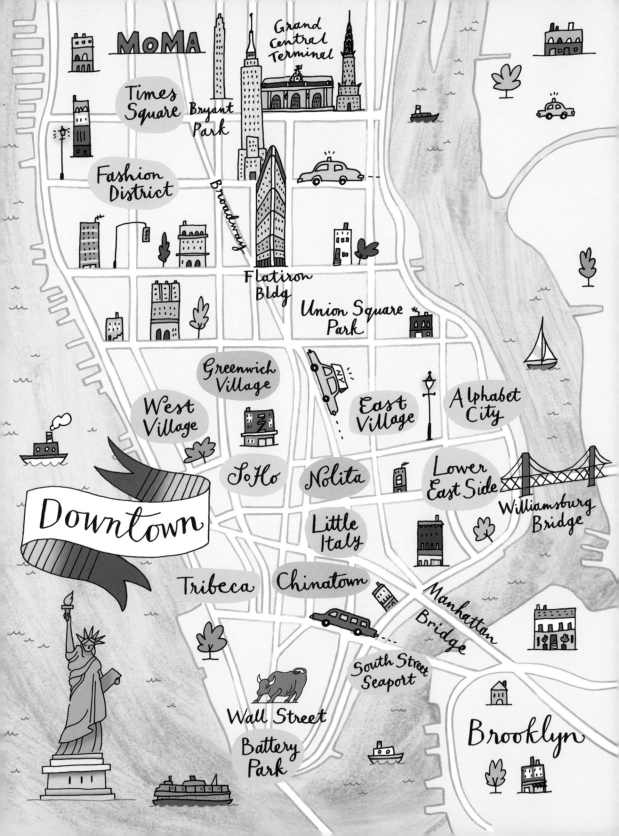

Notes

Columbia University

Studio Museum

Uptown

Harlem

Morningside Park

Central Park

Upper West Side

Upper East Side

Natural History Museum

The Met

Bethesda Fountain

Queensboro Bridge

Midtown West

Midtown East

My Observations while walking across...

BROOKLYN

BRIDGE

People were talking about ...

I love New York because...

My New York City

Photo Album

My New York City

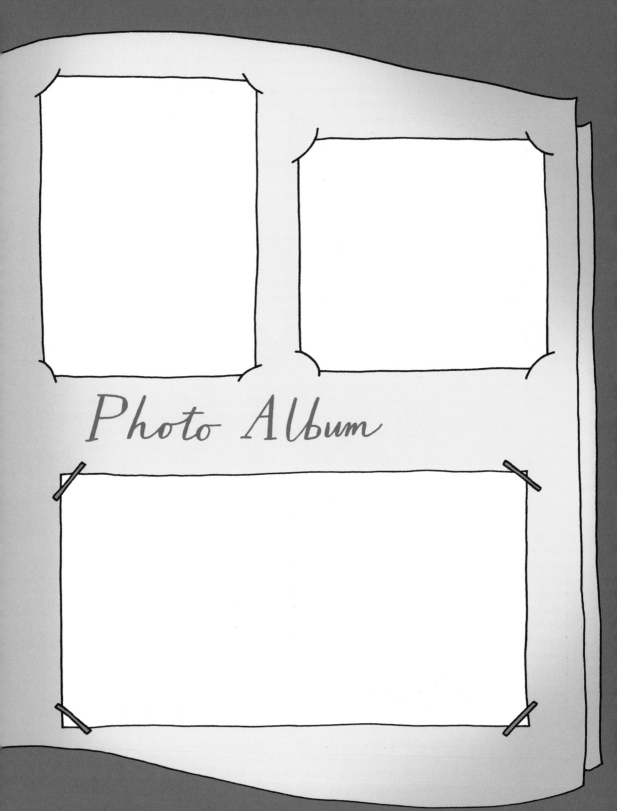

Photo Album

My New York City

Photo Album

What time is it
at Grand Central
Terminal?

Draw your favorite

Draw your favorite

Be inspired
at museums
and try drawing
your own modern
masterpieces ....

Notes and Observations

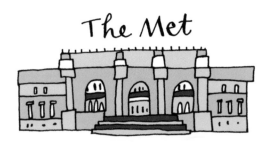

The Met

Activities

Upper East Side

Sites

Restaurants

Shopping

Notes and Observations

Activities

Upper West Side

Sites

Restaurants

Shopping

Notes and Observations

Activities

Harlem

Sites

Restaurants

Shopping

Notes and Observations

Activities

Midtown

Sites

Restaurants

Shopping

Notes and Observations

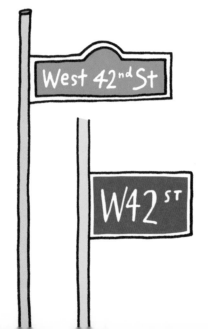

Activities

Times Square

Sites

Restaurants

Shopping

Notes and Observations

Activities

Fashion District

Sites

Restaurants

Shopping

Notes and Observations

Activities

West Village

Sites

Restaurants

Shopping

Notes and Observations

Activities

East Village

Sites

Restaurants

Shopping

Notes and Observations

Activities

SoHo

Sites

Restaurants

Shopping

Notes and Observations

Activities

Little Italy

Sites

Restaurants

Shopping

Notes and Observations

Activities

Lower East Side

Sites

Restaurants

Shopping

Notes and Observations

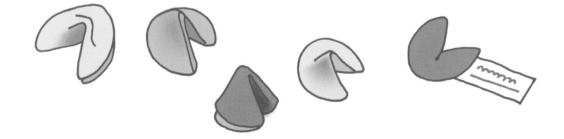

Activities

Chinatown

Sites

Restaurants

Shopping

Notes and Observations

Activities

Downtown

Sites

Restaurants

Shopping

Notes and Observations

Activities

Brooklyn

Sites

Restaurants

Shopping

Notes and Observations

Activities

Sites

Restaurants

Shopping

Notes and Observations

Activities

Sites

Restaurants

Shopping

Central Park

HUDSON RIVER

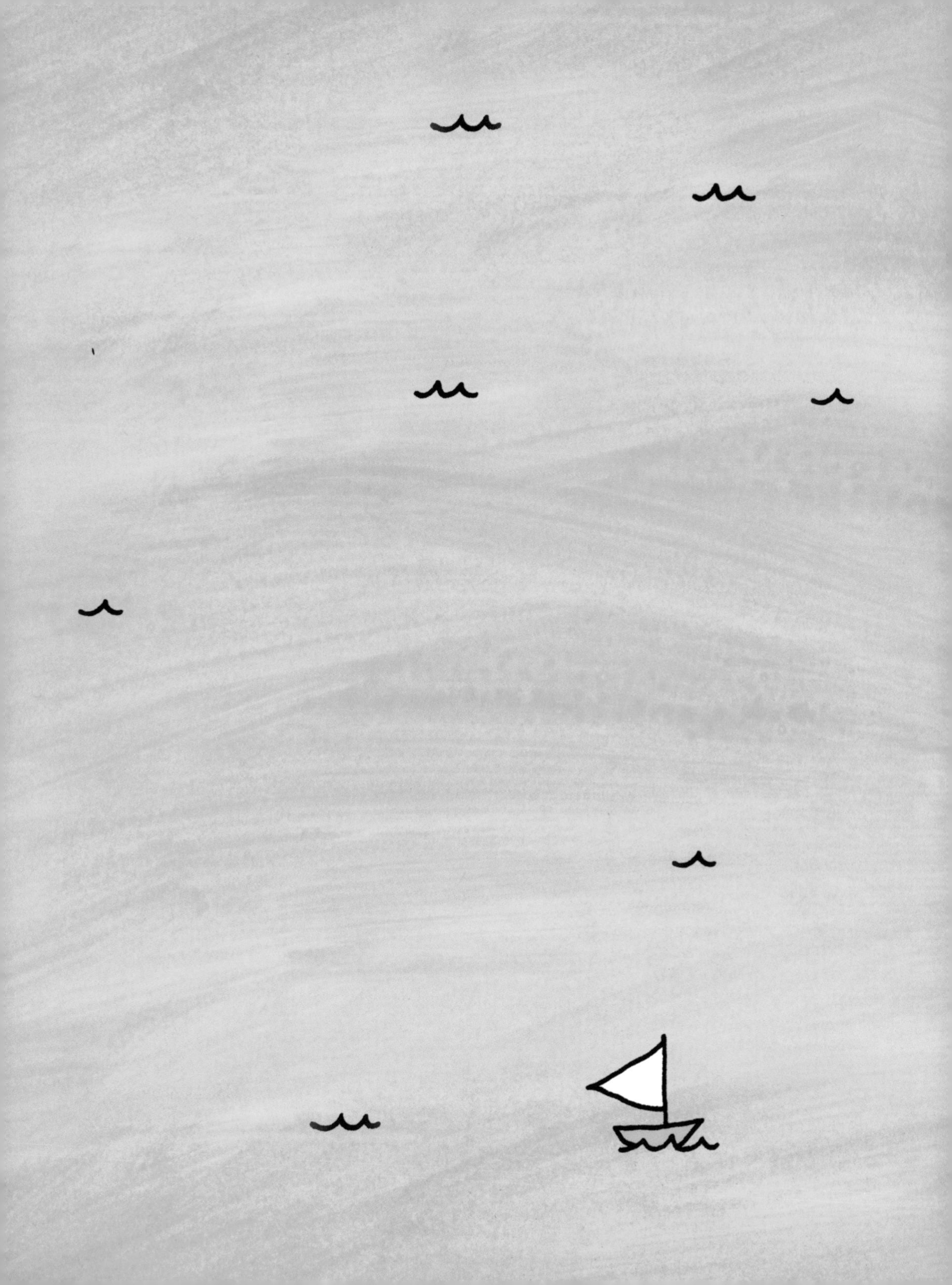

New York City

Sketch

New York City

Explore

I love New York because...

1

2

3

4

5

6

7

8

9

10

Remember

Notes and Observations

Notes and Observations

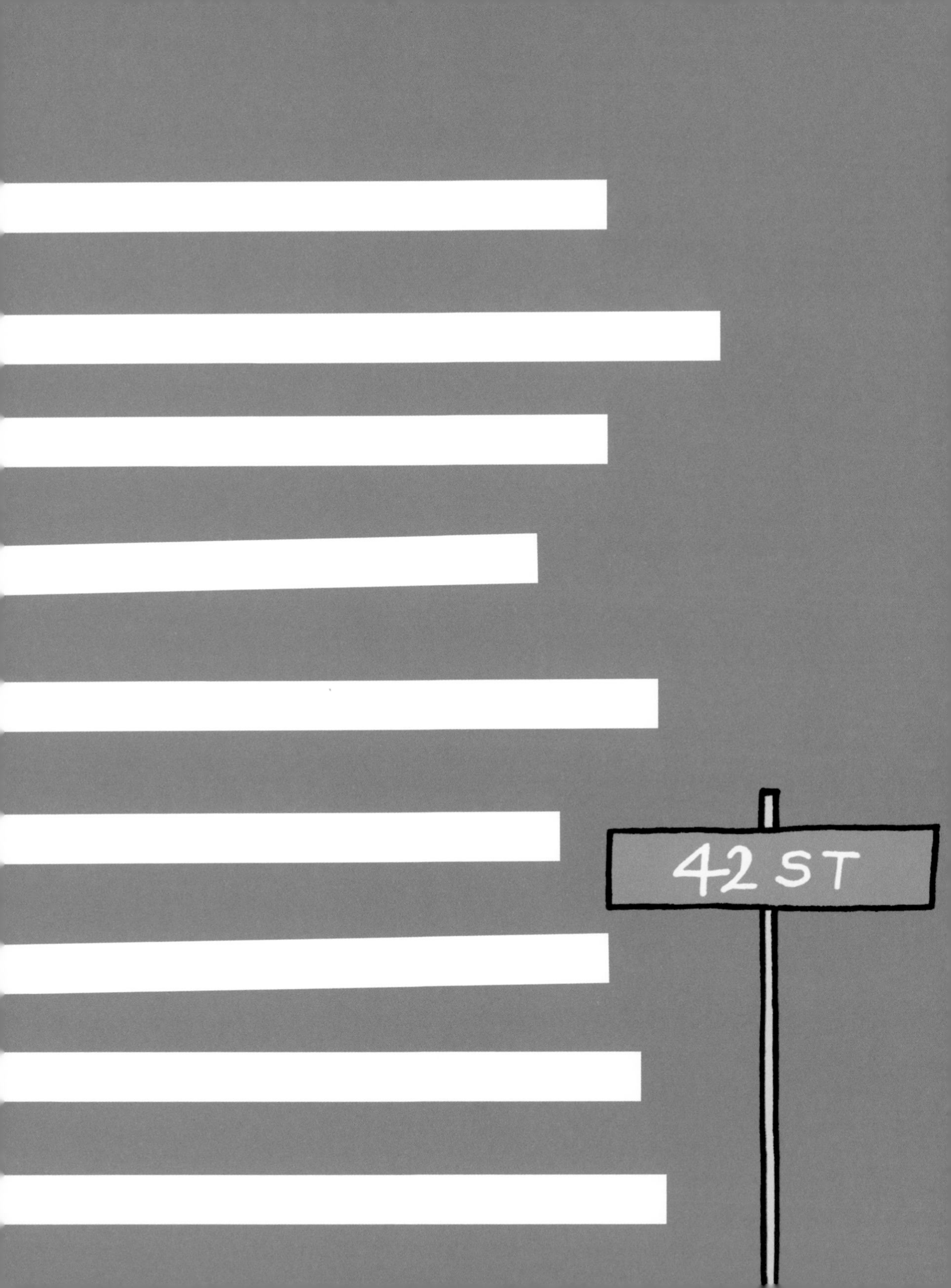
42 ST

Notes and Observations

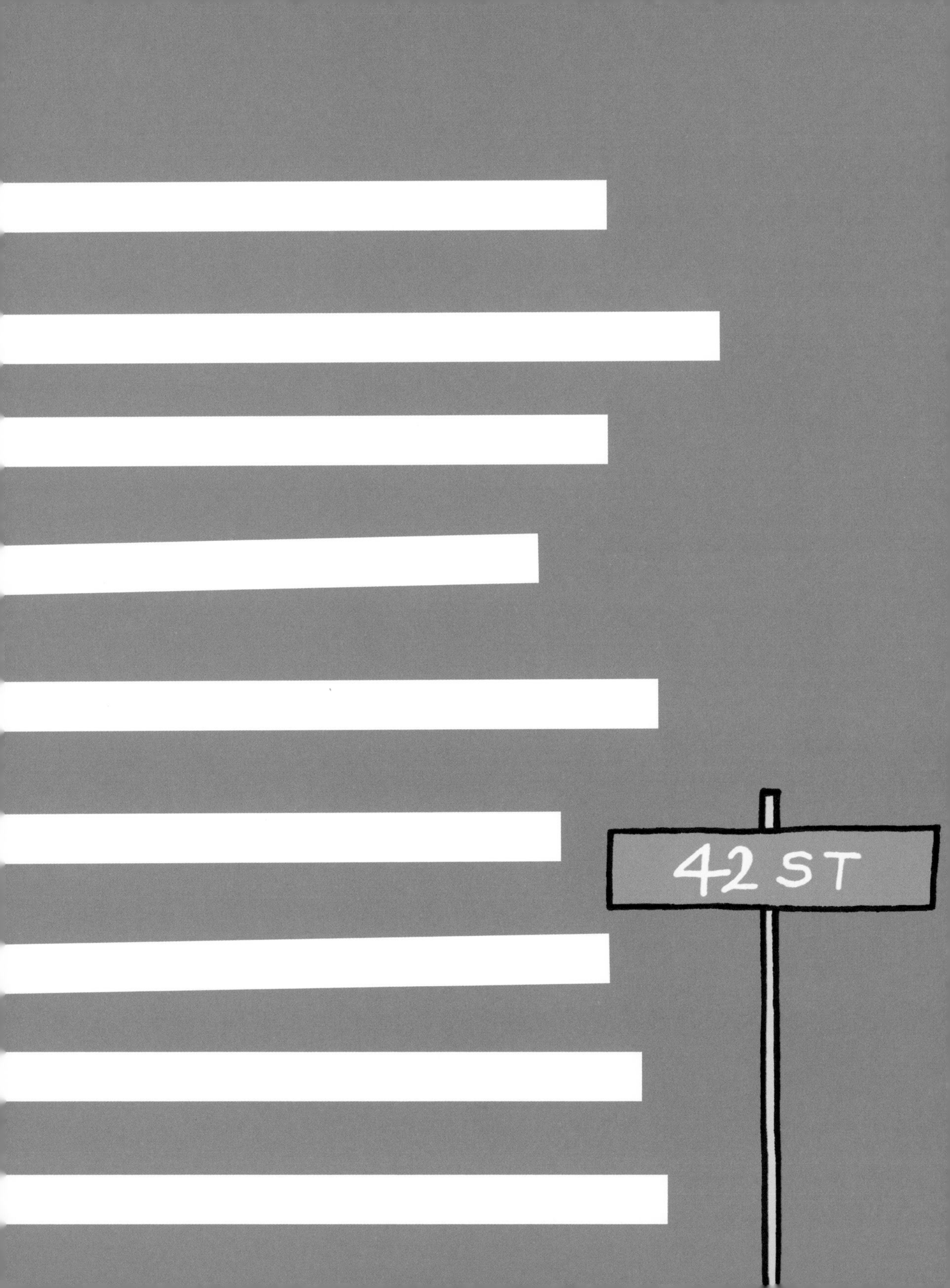
42 ST

Notes and Observations

Record Your Journey

Record Your Journey